at first

DWRG Press

Sea House Studios

photographs by D. Wall

Afterword by Seán Virgo

At first glance… these portraits offer a close-up view of people who, in point of fact, are impossibly distant from us. More than thirty years of day after day has long since transformed them into whatever they were to become. Yet here they are in clear black and white, still mysteriously present. The images in Denis Wall's album expose flashes of tenderness and self-absorption, desire and love, optimism and pain. As you walk these streets with him, you are certain to find yourself in the frame.

- Candace Savage

plates

9

Afterword - The poet George Bowering wrote "A photograph is now and then, now and then."

Now questions Then as we look at Denis Wall's images from the 1980's. Who was he then, the young voyeur stalking the streets of Edmonton? Who is he now, choosing these out of all the possible candidates, and making them public?

And who were these people that he offers us here? Where did they go home to? Who might they be now? What would they see if this book came into their hands, those who still live and might remember?

A posed photograph is a mask – an answer, false or true, to any question we might bring to it. These images begin and end with questions.

There is mischief in Denis Wall's title. A first glance implies a second and demands a third, with the questions that follow and multiply, the answers that may be different each time that we look. Start where you will – the sociology of hemlines or shopping bags; the unselfconscious intimacy of a hand below a breast; the eyes of the ambushed: complicit, affronted, eager, alarmed; the grace and awkwardness of the solitary; the waiting, the hastening. They all make you wonder.
                                                    - Seán Virgo

Artist Statement - You have walked down the street and heard your name called. You have turned and found that you had imagined, the wind speaking to you alone. Whispers from the past. This is a book of spirits; the first of a three-part study of Edmonton streets: 1981, 1997, 2008.

Exploring the hidden is a universal activity, a project of artists, art theorists, natural and social scientists, psychoanalysts, philosophers. Those you met in art classes. It is hermeneutics at best: a weary hunt for a way to clarify meaning. And it is an impossibly flawed undertaking, but fun nonetheless – distracting and consoling at worst.

Today, however, it is time to drop the pretense, to throw away the analytics. Is this irresponsible? Not really. My guess is that structural or social assessments of these photographs, or the book itself, approach the pointless. These images come with no knowledge of who is depicted: pasts, current lives, deaths. These are fictional characters.

Open the book and let that moment of contemplation take you wherever it may. In our world of security extremes and dense politics take this time to relax, to forget hyper-reality and high-definition, to distance yourself from your computer and your phone, to exercise your imagination.

- DW

© 2013 DWRG Press
dwrg@sasktel.net
dwrgpress@gmail.com
Sea House Studios, Box 435, Eastend Sk. S0N 0T0

Library and Archives Canada Cataloguing in Publication

Wall, Denis, 1946-
     At first glance : photographs / by D. Wall ; afterword, Seán Virgo.

ISBN 978-0-9809026-4-8

     1. Edmonton (Alta.)--Pictorial works. 2. Edmonton
(Alta.)--Biography--Portraits. 3. Portrait photography--Alberta--
Edmonton. I. Title.

FC3696.37.W35 2012   971.23'34030222   C2012-901127-4

Printed in Canada

With special thanks to: Sarah, Emily, Caitlin, Alanna, Graham, CEVLHDeC, FED, Lori, Herb, Sharon, Carl, Gina, Hasan, Thomas, Donovan, Brad, and Glenda.

for

Georgia

"Alas, however hard I look, I discover nothing ..." - "I must therefore submit to this law: I cannot penetrate, cannot reach into the Photograph. I can only sweep it with my glance."

Roland Barthes. *Camera Lucida.* NY: Hill and Wang, 1981. P100, 106.

"Today we do not think the virtual, the virtual thinks us."
Jean Baudrillard. *Screened Out.* NY: Verso, 2002. P107.

"... and they could not dream that they were headed at the end of the journey for the boredom of everyday life."

Yukio Mishima. *The Decay of the Angel.* NY: Pocket Books, 1975. P96.